I am Enough

My observations on the journey back to me

Raji

BookLeaf Publishing
India | USA | UK

Made with ❤ on the BookLeaf Publishing Platform
www.bookleafpub.in
www.bookleafpub.com

Dedication

To my dear inner child,

"I am sorry

Please forgive me

I love you

*Thank you."**

I see you, I hear you and I am here for you, always.

You are, and will always be, enough.

*Ho'oponopono

Preface

At the age of seven, I began writing letters and notes to my Dad, who was no longer with us. These weren't just written on scraps of paper torn from my notebook but also as tiny letters visible only to my eyes(and his) inscribed on the yellow wall of my study room with my finely sharpened black HB pencil.

In middle school, I stumbled upon poetry books in our home library. Inspired, I decided to write similar poems of my own, imitating the style of those I admired. My first attempt, a piece about a rose garden, wasn't selected for the school magazine. Undeterred, I dreamt of starting a library and writing stories- dreams that, for a time, faded into the background.

Over the years, my writing habit evolved. From capturing my thoughts and travels in a diary, I moved to jotting introspective "notes to self" and engaging in journaling as a part of self-care routines and "inner work" practices.

During the lockdown, I discovered doodling, a creative outlet that became meditative for me. Drawing to musical sounds brought calm and focus amidst a high-stress lifestyle. It was free-flowing and I grew to love this. Thus, started my daily doodling journey. I am glad to share a few of my doodles in this book, and you can find more on Instagram. @theintuitiveowl showcases more of my work. I'd love to hear your feedback.

Revisiting my diaries from 20 years ago and my journals from recent years inspired me to share my thoughts publicly. The idea of publishing took root, and as if by magic, the opportunity presented itself. And so, this book came to life!

I have come to believe that I am always in the right place at the right time and that the Universe supports me. This exciting new experience feels like the beginning of many more to come. What is meant for you will always find its way to you.

In this book, I share my observations—snippets from life, moments with people who triggered change for the better, reflections on my inner child, memories of flying the nest, musings on infatuation and transactional love, self-discovery, a few amusing thoughts and imagined scenes that sprang from dreams or meditative moments by the ocean in my city.

I am proud of who I am and where I have arrived. I am learning to trust the journey.

Contents

Breaking the Cycle

In complete awareness
I walk back—
consciously,
willingly,
to my roots,
to the past, the blackhole,
the source of all my wounds.

I stand in the presence
of all that I once believed destroyed me.
I am far beyond its reach;
its tentacles can no longer hold me.

Intuition says,
The time is now
to forgive,
to heal,
to let go,
to be thankful,
to bring peace,
to liberate me
from enmeshment,

from unhealthy cycles,
to become a better version of me.

My heart is brimming with love and
compassion,
I am ready to release myself from the past,
I will be the architect of my destiny.

In this journey,
I have worn different masks,
I have been many different versions,
I have been many different women,
I am yet to reach me.

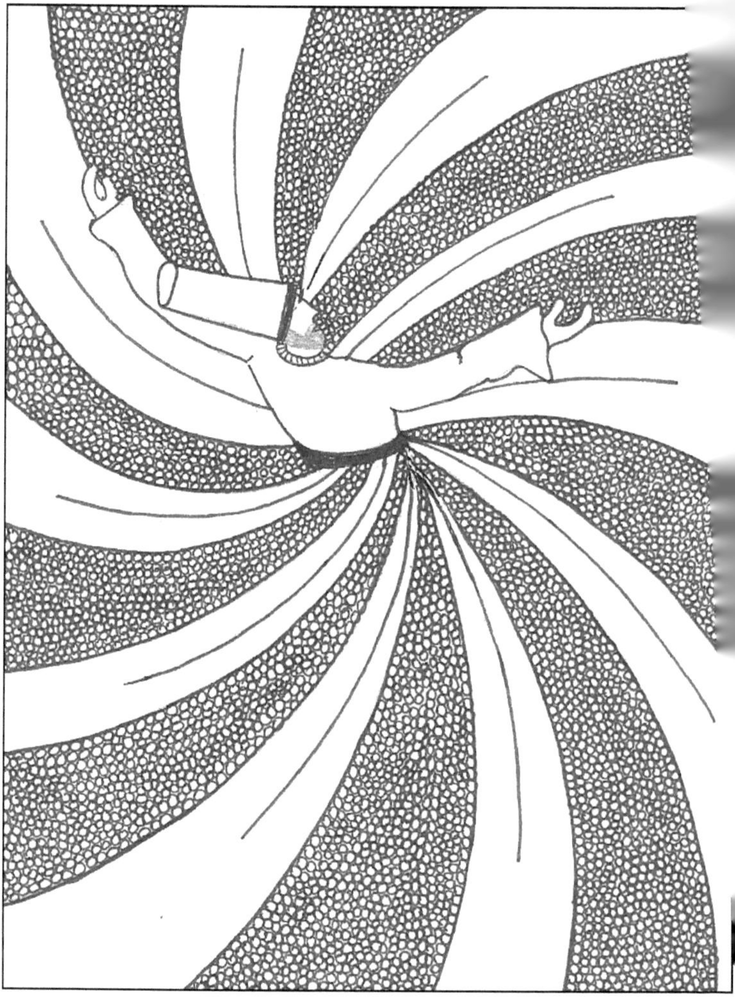

Circles

I kept fighting for love,
I kept testing it.
Chasing,
Craving,
I yearned for it from a source that wasn't me!
It left me in circles
that I keep drawing
and whirling in.
Not like a dervish
unconditionally connecting with the Beloved,
but
like a hamster stuck on a wheel!

Madeleine Moments

Smells-
like keys to forgotten moments
collapse time between the past and the present.
A time machine or Marcel's madeleine-
unleashing ghosts of the past
or playing back
moments that tug at your heartstrings.

Opening my grandmother's closet,
a whiff of naphthalene stirs the past.
I am seven again,
twirling in my favourite frock,
matching shoes and flowers in my hair.

Milk spills on the kitchen counter,
the smell kicks in a memory-
the soft nuzzle of my dog's nose upon my skin,
The smell of her puppy and the
sound of her slurping bits of bread soaked in
milk.

The fragrance of talc powder
whispers the warmth
of the first swaddled newborn
I held in my arms.

The musty smell of old books,
takes me back in time,
to the first library,
where wonder met me as a child.

The fragrance of jasmine blooms-I am ten,
threading flowers into garlands,
with my tender and tiny hands.

The smell of rain,
the earthy scent on the tarred road,
recalls my college days and scooter rides,
returning home through monsoon skies.

We smell before we think,
unpredictably breathing life into the past.

Memories

Memories.
Shrapnel,
lodged deep in elusive recesses.
The mind
battles,
to set them free.

They yearn to flow,
like water seeking the sea.
But lightning strikes,
bitter flashbacks flood the mind.

They lash out,
the heart aches,
deep sobs rise from the pit of the stomach
caught in the rib cage.

A downpour begins,
with a rush of tears,
they break free.

Coherent breathing,
Interrupts your patterns of thinking.
Drifting thoughts,
fleeting sounds,
Don't tail them.

Calmness follows.
no ripples,
no thoughts,
no-mind state,
no more looping memories.

Shift focus!

Seated slyly,
moving swiftly within the iceberg*,
he plays his games—
twisted,
straight,
easy,
upturned.

Apocryphal, enticing, addictive,
he wants you to believe him—
that's how he wins.

Silently, he watches
as you struggle to let go of intrusive ideas.
He keeps you spinning
Swirling thoughts and looping them in
clouding your vision
on this spiraling roundabout.
He seduces you,
with chimeras and meek excuses,
luring you in.

But you spot his trick.
You call him out
The lesson is recognised.
Enlightened,
you know it's time—
to quit,
say *STOP*
To shift focus.
Thank him,
And consciously bow out of his game.

*Iceberg metaphor by Freud

People by the Sea

Lost in his thoughts
at this little seaside shack,
on a bench near me.
Beside him lie
a phone,
AirPods,
and a bunch of keys.
One long gaze,
sadness lingers behind his eyes.
Deep elevens and creases,
a map to a worrier's face
or is there a profound philosopher side to
him?
He is not in his body,
He's detached,
suspended in time.

Hesitant, cautious smiles,
an overthinking mind.
Staring into his laptop screen,
addicted to work,
answering calls, scrolling endlessly,

while sipping on black coffee.
His wounds hold him captive,
he has brushed them all aside.
His tears, a heady mix with Whiskey sour.
He nurses this drink,
lounging on his grey couch.
In his blue tee matched to checked pajamas,
he watches movies and shows
on MUBI and Apple TV+.
His screams
muffled by goose-down pillows
after he switches off the bedside lamp.
Darth Vader boxers,
or Batman sometimes—
and he crawls under the pristine white quilt,
his AC is set to 18 degrees.

Secrets held close, mostly untold.
He stonewalls when you speak with him.
He projects his fears.
Can he trust the man in the mirror
or anyone around him?
He has chosen to
sever the threads of attachment.

How can you
commit a lifetime to just one human being?
Pretending
nothing's wrong,
running from
what he feels.
Lonely.
Searching outside,
hollow within.

He shows his kindness and compassion to all
around him,
never directing it towards him.
He holds a lot of love within,
yet keeps it locked away.
Same same, but different.
Just another flawed human being.
Being human,
like all of us.
It could have been you.
It could have been me.

Reunion

Cold embrace—
ice burns,
no soothing balm.

Words pelted like stones
Irrevocable wounds
that sting deeper
than tincture of iodine.

Memories flogging.
Eidetic.
Etched like ineffaceable tattoos on the mind.

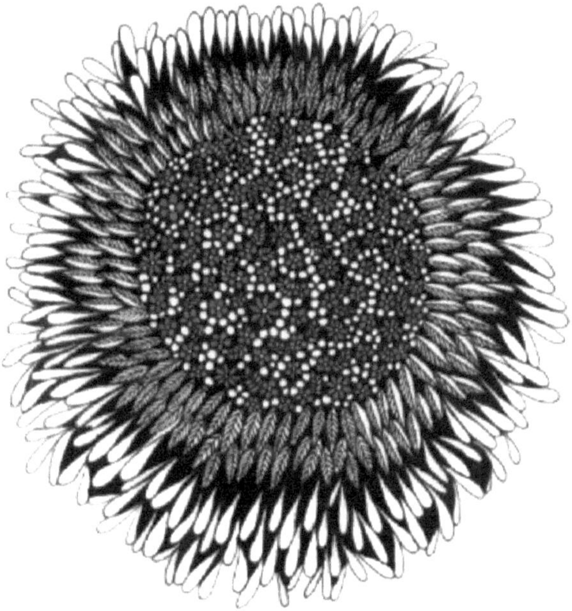

Limerence

And in my dream,
we took to
the winding roads
on a white Lambretta
blue panels,
black seats.
You swerved
through swaying palms,
lush green fields on either side,
along the coconut trees
And beneath Kingfishers perched
on electric wires.
We crossed villages—
children playing seven stones,
abandoned bus stops,

crisp white chapels,
wayside crosses,
up and down,
mounds,
and speed breakers,
and little craters.

Past local schools,
the bustling village market,
baskets of coiled sausages,
strings like rosary beads,
a medley of smells,
cacophony.
We emerge into the open
a gush of fresh air
off the beaten path
zipping towards the sea,
across the river
on the narrowest bridge.
I feel the cool summer breeze.
We share a headphone,
earbud each,
singing to the beat
you turn around
to look at me—

that lopsided smile,
my heart skips a beat.
I'm holding you,
my cheek resting
on your back,
I feel the warmth.
So safe.
So real.
I woke up,
yet still,
We were swerving through
the winding roads.
I feel the warmth—
a dream within my dream.

Self-love

The love I safely carried inside
for years,
to give to another—
still lies here within me.
Unrequited,
I hurt
until I discovered
I could give it all to me.

No longer betraying,
and abandoning who I am,
I pour all that love consciously into me.
Now, all good things flow easily to me.
I am enough.
I choose me.

The Ocean Hurts

Do the waves ever tire?
Does their music ever stop?
Do they fall out of rhythm,
Falter in their step,
or pause for a breath?
Do they feel they need to rest?
Do they long to take a sip of beer?
Munch on potato wafers,
or bite into corn cobs?
Do they secretly desire to lash out at humans?
To fling the bottles,
and all the plastic,
in the faces of those who taint them?

Twisted Love

I said, *Stay away!*
Stay away from me
Keep your distance-
Stand two feet apart.
We are not ready for each other yet,
Don't touch me!

Don't look into my eyes;
they'll hypnotise.
Don't call me by my name;
don't let it linger on your lips.
The vowels will cling,
suck on your tongue,
like a torrid kiss.
There will be no holding back.
you'll reciprocate;
it will all become real.
No longer will it be possible to fool our feelings.
Slaves to carnal desires,
we'll lose ourselves entirely.

My words will titillate,
they'll play on your mind,
brush against your ears,
like passionate ear-licks.
No button to pause,
you'll surely succumb to this hypnotic ear worm,
Impossible to get me out of your head.

Don't save my number,
don't remember my name,
Don't drunk dial, butt-dial,
for if you hear it ring,
my secret will be revealed,
My caller tune,
your favourite song.
The tune on my lips,
matching the sway of my hips,
will drag you in,
your body will struggle,
to fight your logical mind.

Your heart will be wrung,
your craving won't stop.
Irresistible,
Like iron you're pulled
to the magnets of my heart.
We fit perfectly–
matching puzzle blocks,
Or two enzymes,
snugly like key and lock.

Looped into this endless chaotic energy
unable to learn,
to grow,
to heal.
I will take control of you,
command you to confront
your true identity,
and reshape you
into what you resist
and don't wish to be.
Because I believe
in changing everything I see.

And you,
in turn,
will dim my aura, and
drain my energy.
I will feed your ego,
ignore your lack of empathy,
twist myself into a pretzel
to satisfy your every desire.
A slave to my own wounds,
I'll trigger you.
I'll drench you in a love you'll never witness in
any of your lifetimes.
I'll crave validation,
No sense of self,
I sacrifice
Till I wear out and wither with time,
And fly around as ashes and dust
and be no longer visible to any naked eye.
I'll ruin you
I'll discard you
I'll abandon you
I'll first wait for you to love me
just so I can hate you.
I need to save you from yourself.
Save me, from you.

And you from me!
A dilemma!
Twisted love.

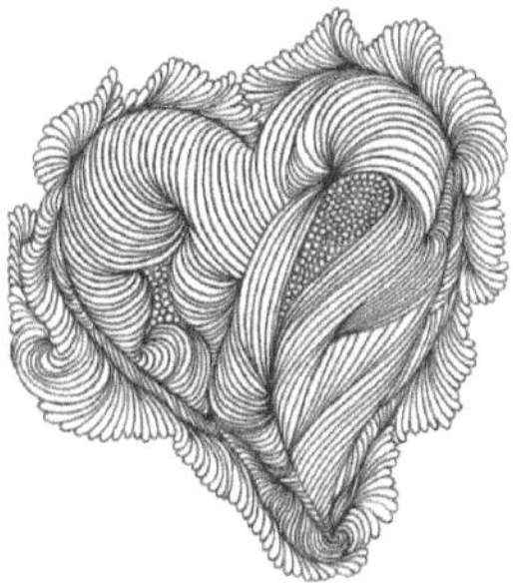

I said, "Stay away!
Stay away from me!"

School

Memories, are we?
Some memories stay,
and some fade away...
Are we just memories
at the end of our day?
Are we no more than a sum of
what we've seen,
and what we've felt?
You, my memory.
Me, a memory to you.

Do we arrive in groups,
interacting only within them?
We seem categorised,
forming specific connections,
relationships defined.
We fleet through a lifetime
in each other's reality,
we either remain
or drift away?

I gained admission
to this school,
a decision solely my own.
A uniform called the body,
one I chose to wear everyday.
Each person
I meet facilitates an experience,
a lesson.
At times, a compass,
a guide, a teacher,
all while I journey
the road back to me.

I don't have that Template!

Her fancy-ass parents
reject her love for her boyfriend,
to find her a boy
of their social standing.
This could be love.

She secretly nurtures
the love-child in her womb,
carries her for nine months,
only to abandon her,
give her up to an eager couple
for a better life.
This could be love.

The narc couple
raise this innocent child—
torture her, yet pamper her
with the best of everything.
This could be love.

She is blinded by love for someone,
He frees her from abuse.
But he assaults her very being.
This could be love.

She meets a stranger,
feels a connection that could last forever,
but he rejects her,
leaving to continue his journey.
This could be love.

She tends to her invalid tormentor,
endures nightmares for years,
and still feels unseen.
This could be love.

No right programming,
no script for love,
her love language
was to keep seeking it outside
until she finally explored within.
This could be love.

How do you know love?
I don't have that template!
Do you know what love is?

The Life of Another

At times,
I turn around,
looking back into my past life.
The years have slipped away,
wrinkles have set in,
The child has grown—
both outwardly and within.

I'm glad it's over—
the pains and the pasted smiles,
the highs and lows
of a masked, fake life.
It feels as if it belonged to someone else,
someone I once knew closely.
At times,
I feel like I am peeping
into a magic crystal ball,
rewinding, replaying,
memories suddenly well up,
of a life gone by
only to slowly blur and fade away.

No signs of pain,
no repentance,
just lessons learnt.
Some scars remain,
It all seems like
an out-of-body experience—
surreal.
But, I am right here right now,
creating and living
my new reality
Acknowledging where I've arrived.
I am the new version.
And that was
the life of another,
the one I wasn't born to be.

Am I My Own Ally?

Who is my ally?
Am I my own ally yet?
Who is this kind soul
urging me to not repeat the same pattern,
pulling me back from stepping into survival mode?
And who is the other one,
Constantly pushing me
back onto the hamster wheel,
and telling me how comfortably familiar
and thrilling the ride will be.

Who are these two, locked in their struggle to control me?
Who am I?
Where am I in all of this?
Which one is me?

Parentified

I was born to be a parent
I seemed to be a natural
I was an excellent multi-tasker
Flawless under high pressure
I could manage and control everything
around me
I felt powerful as a young girl
And I was so proud of it.

I was born to be a mother before I was even a
child
I was assigned to care, to be the confidant,
the therapist, the listener,
the good friend,
their ego boost,
the nurturer of others' inner children
and help them meet their needs
and wipe out all of mine.

I grew up without a stable identity,
I couldn't develop a complete sense of self
I didn't know better.

Instead, I floated through fantasies.
In my mind, I wove beautiful fairy tales.
I lost the flow.
I wandered around for lifetimes within a lifetime,
until a day dawned,
my eyes opened,
my brain jump-started.
It's wiring restored,
ready to move out from autopilot zombie mode.

A new desire sparked–
to bloom
and the eagerness to grow
pushed me to look for more
I needed to be the creator,
to no longer live
on borrowed dreams,
borrowed goals,
a borrowed life.

My body
was already exhausted,
sabotaged by itself.

My butterfly gland busted.
The cells worn out and torn,
attacked each other
by mistake
when I was a child.
My life had been resonating
in unfamiliar planes,
low energies,
no balance,
off-center.
I had forgotten to breathe,
it felt like narcosis underwater
diving in the dark, in the deep.

My mind fogged,
my body froze when all of a sudden
I heard an echoing voice
telling me that I wasn't being myself.
I was drawn towards it,
to explore this thought,
to pull myself out,
from my sinking life.
I read and reread,
and devoured many books
of varied subjects.

Curious, investigating like a detective,
to retrieve this gem, my hidden self.

Transitioned to hermit mode,
I was drawn to meet kind enlightening souls,
urged to study the self,
I danced, I sang,
drew on paper, listened to sounds,
At times, I withdrew into silence
to dive within and extract me out.

It felt like ascent
from the bottom of murky waters.
I plunged out for air,
the moment had arrived.
Wholeheartedly, with clarity
I knew it was time to seize this life.
I took long breaths...
Breathe in.
Breathe out.
Not through my mouth.
I now learnt it right.
Breathing in
through my nose,
filling my stomach and exhaling out.

This time consciously,
and in rhythm
activating the energy within, I was back.
I felt everything in me.
Though nature and circumstances still shake me,
Though I do slip and slide,
I pull myself up each time.
I'm centered and steady
through focus, through breath.
I returned to the center smoothly and swiftly.
I let go of the noose,
I thought it was strangling me.
I now know I am safe,
I am myself
No longer a mother, no longer a father,
No longer a role imposed by others
I am simply me.
I see myself,
I feel free.

My Dear Inner Child

I held her hand
and led her through
the darkest tunnels
that had blurred her life.

Self-sabotaged,
her feelings dead,
her tear ducts shut,
until she got a glimpse of light.

I hugged her tight
to show her warmth.
I listened to her,
watched the tears burst out and flow.

I embraced all of her,
acknowledged her emotions.
Her beliefs were so strong,
she struggled to let go.

She was alone and lost,
this little whimpering child
tucked in a little corner
in a faraway world.

She has been found
She resides with me now
I am reparenting her,
I am her everything.

I keep her safe.
She is my priority and
the one I love and respect.
My dear inner child.

Only You Know Your Truths

The way you have fears,
not visible to the outside world,
I have shadows just as vile,
they gnaw me from inside,
just like they feast on you.
The ego, blind and stubborn
failed to acknowledge them,
concealing their chaos,
from my sight and yours too.
I spot, I nudge
these trickster imps
before they run amok
and sabotage my choices like they always do.

I flash a spotlight on them—
blind spots,
stage fright.
They know, I know
They squiggle,
they say they've been my saviors
and my armor too.

Yet, I see them for what they are,
I replay how they pulled my strings
and messed with my authentic story.
The truth flashes in front of me
The unconscious magically turns
conscious.
Weakened,
fading,
they cannot maneuver me through the same
old pathways,
I have chosen to release these fears.
Awakened from deep slumber,
emerging from the cocoon,
eyes wide open,
illuminating the dark,
revealing the golden side
I allow myself to integrate the fragmented
parts of me.

Shame

Dear Universe,
Give me some magic beans,
Send me angels with soothing balm,
a wand to swish and flick,
and some magic spells
to dissolve this shame I hold within me.
This shame sowed by others,
passed down through generations—
to and from my mother,
my grandmothers
and all their ancestors.
This deep-rooted burden weighs heavy within
me
Please, free my body from the pain of it all.
It presses on my neck,
hunches my shoulders,
I hang my head low, I stumble over words.
How do I shed this "soul-eating emotion"?
How do I connect with myself?
How do I pluck out this poison and break its
flow?

Guide me to show more compassion for
myself.
Bring me loving experiences that bring out
the calm in me,
and make me want to love me more.

Shadow Puppetry

And when we met
The sun was up in its balcony seat,
The full moon was sad to miss bathing us
in her silvery light.
The ocean was eagerly leaping
and lapping the shore, waiting to see us meet.

We climbed up to cross the bridge,
to step onto the sand carpet that led to the
waters.
Strolling and exchanging pleasantries,
he stooped down to watch
the Bubbler crab making sand pellets and
scurrying across to burrow and hide.
I, facing the sea, enjoyed the breeze,
unbuckling and setting aside my
black Nappa leather thong sandals.
Bare feet,
my toe tracing tiny nervous squiggles
on one spot
on this vast stretch of golden beach.

While the sun danced on my
glossy, burgundy-streaked hair,
his eyes traced my Grapefruit-pink lips,
nifty maneuver, straight into my eyes,
I felt the current travel to my feet.
The prancing waves tried to play
“running and catching” and “tag you're it!”
while our shadows danced behind us,
meeting,
conspiring,
so discreet,
as though they had a million secrets to share.
Treated like puppets,
we displayed
unfiltered erratic behaviour,
oblivious to their antics.

Our dark twins took over
as we sat down in a café
to sip on our drinks and speak.
Naïve, childlike,
we thought we were meeting alone,
but we weren’t, in reality.

As two transactional humans,
we triggered each other,
overthinking quietly.
We haven't met our own selves in reality.
We are unable to ignore the matrix.
The shadow side of him meets the shadow
side of me.
We carry along our shadows, unintegrated.
Our meeting—
it wasn't you, it wasn't me.
We still haven't met
without the dark shadow side of you, and the
darkest shadow side of me.

*Inspired by Carl Jung's Shadow concept

Finding Stillness

Lucid dream.
In an abyss,
tentacles of the past
lure me
into the deep,
waiting to suck my soul,
waiting to drain the breath from me—
akin to the Dementor's kiss.
But I am beyond its reach.
I am calm.
I stand up for me.
A cocoon of white light shields me.
I am the most aligned I have ever been.

The Love I Seek Outside

I always looked for love
I did!
As a child,
I searched for love
in every nook and corner.
In candlelight, under moonlight,
in every little doggie,
in every living being,
behind laughter,
in smiles, behind every sign,
in Archie's cards,
Or
in the letters written to me—
just in case their love was scribbled in
invisible ink.
In my favorite cuisine and seafood dishes,
or in the chocolate chip cookies baked fresh
for me.

I looked for love
in a genuine kiss from an aunt
that left a red lipstick print on my chubby cheek.
This beautiful stain, I refused to erase or wash it away.

I looked for love
in a warm hug from a granny
that left Chanel No 5 lingering on my skin.
This floral fragrance, this essence of love, I never wanted it to fade.

I looked for love
in endearing names like Pinky and Dolly,
and in flattering statements,
not for my academics or skills, but
for my complexion and skin tone, or my thick long lustrous hair.

I looked for love
in marriage proposals whispered at family gatherings,
and in love notes from sweet boys
asking to meet by our school gate.

But as a teenager,
I turned down good men
and fine families
who showed their love
in a thousand different ways.

Each day, I added one important task in my checklist—
the only one that never got a tick at the end of each day:
"Scan for love. Find love"
I would carry it forward sincerely to the next day,
I always looked for love outside,
I looked for love each day.

The funny part is,
that the love I was looking for
I could not recognize it.
I didn't know what it should look like
or what it should be or could be,
even if it stood right in front of me.
It almost seemed like I wasn't in the right queue at the start of school
when they were doling out notes about it.

Maybe I missed the school bus on that
particular day and no staff cared to check on
me or let me into this big secret.
Maybe it had 50 chapters and I missed the
gigantic textbook which held a thousand
pages,
as I always disliked reading nonfiction,
or fiction that's greater than 450 pages.
This subject of love wasn't even offered to me
later,
not even as an elective,
Had it been,
I would have willingly opted to study it.
I was excellent at learning by rote, I could
parrot anything that was read or said.
With my photographic memory, I would have
flipped pages, flipped the book front to back,
back to front,
behind my closed eyes, in my mind's eye,
scan pages,
pick out the right lines and words,
translate them into habits and behaviours and
put these notes on love into practical use.
But the world didn't teach it like I needed it
to.

The world,
these love teachers,
these primary caregivers
seemed so unfair to the little child in me,
So I had to tutor myself, make mistakes,
take tests,
gamble choices,
to shape myself and create a fresh reality!

Beautiful Lies

Just fooling yourself,
not accepting your reality.
Resisting life lessons.
More beautiful were the lies.

The child believed he could leap to catch the
moon.
He was convinced he could snatch the stars
from the black sky.
Innocence.
More beautiful were the lies.

Runaway Girl

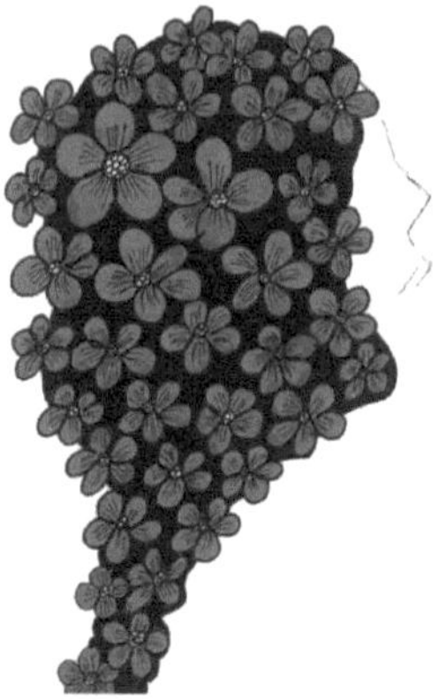

The astrologers
map the stars in the sky,
track the planets in their orbits,
and capture the magical moment of her arrival
on Earth.
Equipped with this cosmic blueprint,
they confidently decipher and declare what lies
ahead,
pleasing the hands that shower them with silver
coins in exchange for her story.

She will be a doctor,
work and live across the seven seas.

She will be a philosopher,
guiding and shaping lives.
She will be a good wife,
bring luck to her man,
and bear him two boys, no girls.

The family soothsayer said,
"She is an old soul,
with a glow on her face and a spark in her eyes.
She will be successful and wise.
Defying all authority,
she will leave home, for she is a mismatch in
your family tree."

In her growing-up days,
these found families called her names,
called her a useless Jack-of-all-trades.

She learnt to play small;
her talents and academic excellence
insignificant in their eyes.
She thought her skin was dark,
and her nose was not straight enough.

They bullied and ridiculed her, and confused her each day.

In her big little world,
overpowering adults, disguised as protectors and guides,
carved paths for girls:
Marriage was a goal,
then bearing a child.
They programmed brains and hypnotized young minds
with horse-blinkers on innocents that they
weren't good enough for anything else,
even before they could discover themselves.

She was pushed to take matters into her own hands.
She decided to just be herself,
a runaway.

Waiting

I watch.
People sitting on a bench by the sea,
waiting...
for the waves to rise and touch their feet.

Waiting...
for their phone to ring,
for the good news of a new life on earth,
for someone to meet you by appointment,
for another's disappearance from your life,
or for someone to launch your enemy into
space.

Waiting...
for a job,
for love,
for the perfect man,
for the perfect woman,
for an even better partner,

for that child who will take forward your
surname, extending your lineage,
or for others to provide meaning to your void
life.

Waiting...
for people,
for closure from another,
for the right time,
for the wrong time to pass,
for fears to dissolve,
for someone to save you from your dark side,
for sleep to kiss your eyes on sleepless nights,
for your nightmares to take a pause,
for your dreams to turn true,
or for someone to hold you
and drive away your blues.

But,
those you are waiting for are unaware
of what you're putting yourself through,
For they may be waiting for someone else too!
Living life in limbo,
lost in time,

the years slip by,
until you wake up one day like I did, introspect
and realize why.

Maybe, this waiting began
when you were little
trying to balance yourself
on the large swinging gate of the house,
waiting for someone to catch you from
slipping.
Or when you were fumbling on the pedal and
falling down learning to ride a bicycle, waiting
for your father to appear, hold the carrier and
give it a soft push.
Or when you sat by the doorstep dreaming, fell
ill with a fever,
or never ate for a day, just played around with
food on the plate. Waiting!
Waiting for father and mother to show up,
their absence led you to continue to wait,
and while waiting,
you wove the most beautiful fairy tales.
They were real and so perfect.

And so you creatively discovered a myriad ways
to draw attention to yourself.
Waiting...
for someone to see you,
to validate you.
And so,
You sought in others
What you couldn't see in yourself.

Rumination

Rewind, recall.

The bits and bytes of every memory.

No real you,

no real me.

It's all in our minds.

Choose the illusion

you wish to see.

Alter Ego

I met the love of my life
after a long break.
He smashed my heart
to smithereens,
they are still lying there on the floor,
unsure if they will be put back together again.

I return home and sit in my room,
I feel like I am watching myself in a projected
movie,
playing out smoothly from a spool, 8mm film,
no sound,
but it rolls out with complete clarity.

Of course, I am the main heroine,
playing the role of a tragedy queen.
I suffer from heartbreak,
and somewhere deep inside I am doing a little
jig,
and rejoicing in this sadness.
I watch me peek into the mirror,

I shock myself,
I look so stunning dressed in black and white,
the kohl-rimmed eyes have just the right bit of
black,
a slight smudge.
And the rhythmic movement of the shrugging
shoulders,
the body, the long delicate fingers wiping the
eyes,
holding the chin of this small, tender face,
makes this soundless sob look so tragically
beautiful.
The movements are fluid
like 'Maya' water, Arabic dance step.
I follow the tears that well up and flow down,
streaming down my stained cheeks and lips,
imaginarily tuned to some kind of lilting
music.

Feeling all sad for myself
keeps me safe and comfortable,
that's the program I am so familiar with,
pushing away people easily,
just content living in this dream,

and not in the reality of being with him.

Like box office projections,
I was so sure of my prediction, the moment
this rom-com began.
This movie wouldn't move forward,
it would be tragic in parts, like a "Romeo and
Juliet".
I am so well-attuned to danger,
hyper-vigilant,
fear will take over by default.
I always know what's coming ahead,
and yet I go forward, throw myself in front of
the approaching train or jump like the
matadors in Sevilla, to tame the roaring wild
bull in the bullring.
I know I am doomed to a violent, bloody
heartbreak.

I continue watching me,
waiting for the last tear drop to fall,
slipping in and out of sad emotions,
and for the overflowing buckets to stop.

But then I am intrigued by what's playing
before me,
I have forgotten about the heartbreak,
forgotten the tears,
and even the man in the real world who is
contradictory
to the man held in the mind, inside my head.
I am watching me stand in front of the mirror,
enthralled by my looks,
facial expressions and emotive skills,
and preparing myself for the next Act.
Am I meant to be a female Kabuki artist in
blue makeup
to symbolise what I am going through?
I long to play a role similar to other
protagonists of my choice,
maybe,
the pomegranate blossom from historical
fiction, Anarkali,
or Francesca pining for Robert Kincaid in
"The Bridges of Madison county",
while I also daydream of being Leslie with
Bach, in "The Bridge Across Forever" in an
alternate world.

I cling to the desire of finding true connection,
although tragedy and doubt run in my veins.
Is someone out there, actually made for me?
Does he exist there already?
Does tragedy elevate the romance in the eyes of
others and within ourselves
and make it adventurous and memorable?
It does sound cruel and sadistic,
but the greatest romances are said to be
tragedies!
Addicted to tragedy,
interspersed with moments of sweet love,
so wicked to thyself,
triggering the dark side in a loop,
this is how mechanical and wicked one can be!
I am guilty of being so wicked to me!

The Blue I see

Just like you have a story,
I have mine too.
We can exchange notes,
on who had it better,
was it me, or was it you?

"Is the blue I see, the same blue that you see?"

Use Her!

Use her!
Use her as your mirror,
when she shows herself to you.
What you see in her,
and all that you see around, are mere reflections of you.

Witness how, with each brush of your sensitive wound,
you pull up a shield to deflect, assuming an attack on you.
Ramped up like a stop-motion video,
brick by brick, a fortress builds up rapidly and locks you in, to protect you.

We live in a house of mirrors, funhouse images too.
All that triggers you, leads you to the unhealed parts,
and to the deepest beliefs,
you have stored in you.

I am a reflection of what you allow me to be.
I see inspiration, trust, peace, abundance and
love around me.
Tune in to see it in all your reflections too.
I deserve to experience the best version of you.

Diary Entries of an Unhealthy Story.

11:30 pm, Friday, Oct 30, 2xxx
At a pub,
Intoxicated and high.
That bright smile
I could have drowned in his eyes,
while I was confident
he slipped and fell into mine.

7:30 pm, Saturday, Nov 4, 2xxx
You seem like an addict.
I am an addict too.
You drink to numb the pain;
I just dream of you.

10:30 pm, Saturday, Nov 11, 2xxx
When eyes met eyes
A sea of thoughts emerged.
Our feelings could not be disguised.

11:30 pm, Friday, Dec 8, 2xxx
My eyes always spoke;
you chose not to listen.

11:30 pm, Friday, Jan 19, 2xxx
We both. Electrified.
My soul interpreter caught in
the web of your
lustful eyes!

4:30 pm, Sunday, Feb 18, 2xxx
Party.
As we slow danced,
I wished the music would never fade.

We are two attention seekers,
entangled-
the pull of desire, the push to flee.

9:30 pm, Saturday, Mar 17, 2xxx
Dinner.
If these old walls of my home could speak of
my perfect life and masked faces,
my secrets would be revealed.
Struggling to breathe, I am unable to contain
them within.

6:30 pm, Saturday, Jun 15, 2xxx
Movie.
Other heartaches took over
masking your absence.
That eye-lock lingered,
We'd never cross paths again.

7:00 am, Wednesday, Jan 14, 2xxx
Bustling city,
full of high energy.
300-year-old hamlet,
crooked, narrow lanes.
Charming cottages in a fishing village,
with the smell of the sea in the air.
Pigeons perched on the tin rooftop,
cacophony outside.

Two bodies,
lost in thoughts,
silence hangs heavy between them.
The pillow of desire, crushed with fear and doubt.
A complex dance, mixed emotions.
One body filled with silent wrath,
the other buried in shame.

1:15 am, Friday, Nov 7, 2xxx
How do I erase you from the depth of my soul?
How do I break this contract that I signed alone?
How do I forget the slow dance of our "burning souls"?
How do I let go?

6:00 pm Saturday, Oct 22, 2xxx
I forgot to forget you.
Here we are,
two strangers.
The past personified before me.

10:00 am Sunday, Oct 23, 2xxx

You were my mirror.

If I hadn't met you then,

I wouldn't have found me.

What triggers you, teaches you!

Change

One of us has to change.
One of us has to heal.
Let it be me.

I am trying to be the change that I have been constantly seeking.

Teenagers

It's his 15th birthday.
I dash down the cobbled street,
after my ballet class,
for his birthday treat with friends,
at a brand-new café round the school block.

"Romeo and Juliet" by Tchaikovsky still
playing in my head.
My short black hair held back with my tiara,
a wreath of little flowers and ivory baby's
breath.
Blush mink leotards,
matching pointe shoes,
12 layers of tulle in my skirt, a neat little tutu.
I carry my red sling pouch,
housing my heart I wear so flimsily,
while tiny pink hearts animatedly dance
around my head.
If I did the MBTI test in Korea,
I would waltz between ISFP, INFJ, and ENFJ
personalities.

A sweet smile on my soft lips,
oh, so ready to please!
A twirl in my step,
I could do 11 pirouettes,
to wipe the sadness away,
and iron out the frown that lingers on his face
to this day!

I stream into a dream.
He will be...
The one I would sing duets with,
circling the columnar eucalyptus trees of Ooty.
We'll be at the cinemas watching Val Kilmer in
"The Saint",
and he will spring me a surprise by going down
on one knee
before the red velvet stage curtain rises
dramatically.
Confessing his never-ending love for me, we'd
watch the movie,
sharing pure joy and popcorn from one big
paper tub!

We will walk into the sunset holding hands, like
the end of Indian movies.
It was clearly a huge crush,
two- sided, one- sided,
who cares?
I had let myself float aimlessly, mindlessly.

Towering over me, staring into my face, stood
this tall, lanky nerd,
adjusting his black, thick horn-rimmed
spectacles.
Back from my reverie, I am blushing.
"Happy birthday,"
I wish him the best, excited and fidgety.
I then dip my hand into my red sling pouch,
ready to give him the surprise gift, my heart,
the one I wear so flimsily.
Disinterested he seems.
He behaves like he doesn't deserve it.
I ruminate for a bit.
What has he done to earn it?
Will he squander it?
My brain plays it out first.

In an alternate life, I would have handed it over
without a thought.

I am jolted back to my senses,
I listen to him thank me,
make an excuse, and then scoot away.

It's another year, another birthday.
I seem to be unable to erase the memory of the
date.
I have baked him his favourite carrot cake.
And so, I run down the cobbled street
for his birthday treat with friends
at the same café!
He blows out the 18 candles and cuts the cake.
Adjusting his black, thicker horn-rimmed
glasses,
he stares down into my face.
"Happy birthday,"
I wish him the best.
He speaks to me, he is still 15 today.
Disappointed,
feeling very sad, I ran down my path,

back home.
I dance for myself.
I pirouette.
Friends, and yet not.
He is free.
I am free.
Life goes on.
We have made our choices clearly, at least for today.

Love Language

I calligraph little notes,
tucking them in your beige linen shirt pocket.
You find them later,
on your ride to the airport.

You send me notes,
music files you created for me,
while you were busy at a conference overseas.

I throw you glances,
through gaps between heads in a crowded
room.
You catch them swiftly, and volley them back
to me.

I speak to you in shapes and designs,
inked in circles and lines.
No cryptanalyst could ever decode.

Sitting on the sand, sundowners by the sea,
I squint my eyes,
I catch you watching me.

At the supermarket, my origami grocery list,
for you in your green pants pocket.
Treasure hunt.
You smile. Reading between the lines,
interspersed with tiny hearts and clues.

Detaching with Love

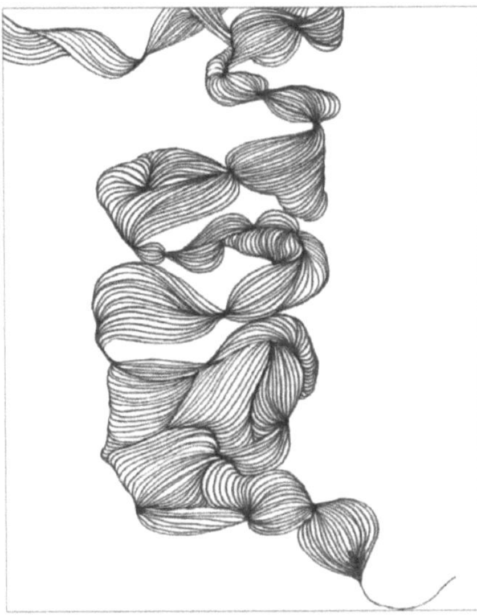

I am at peace,
with the choices you make,
for your mind, body, and soul.
I am not
invested in you changing.
I honor you,
I honor me,
and I set myself free.

Girls are Goddesses

I saved myself while you attempted to get rid of me,
Did you not realise that I was still alive?
I heard all your poison-tipped words,
while I was cozily tucked inside,
growing perfectly,
waiting for my time to explore the world.
Instead of hearing sweet lullabies,
or you speaking to me with that beautiful voice,
all that fell on my delicate ears
were the cruel plans your companion was hatching.
I know all the options you thought of to get rid of me.
I could sense your fears, your thoughts,
and the ugly emotions you went through,
while you forgot I was embedded deep inside you.
I wanted to kick you hard with all my might,
but you thought it was a nudge,

I was just a tiny, innocent pea of a child.
When the time arrived for me to be welcomed,
to witness the miracles of earth, of life,
to view this universe and to be in your arms,
I was whisked away from beneath your nose.
You had an inkling of feeling to keep me with
you,
but your actions didn't match your feelings.
Sweet abandon, like I was a soiled nappy in the
clothes basket!
You selfish woman, did you think you'd have a
better life without me?

You will be shocked to know that I made it
and,
I live with a beautiful home and family,
I am alive!
Breathing, living and enjoying the wonders of
the world outside!
Maybe I chose you, for a lesson you had to
learn through me and me through another.
Sometimes, I wonder if you would be happy to
know,
that this "Goddess" has survived.

More than 30 TB

Feeling low.
Flip. Flip. Flip.
Scouring through the library of files in my
drive,
32 TB into a hundred trillion times.
I've chosen to pick out a memory to relive
today.
It's a fake!
At times, the mind, in the absence of evidence,
or to fill in the gaps, assumes many things.
It can create a story, to make sense of what is
happening.
I am a storyteller,
I created it to lift me up when I feel I am
slipping down.
I've played it a million times,
and now it seems so real.
It holds me, it soothes me,
a quick dopamine shot,
it helps to keep me happy.

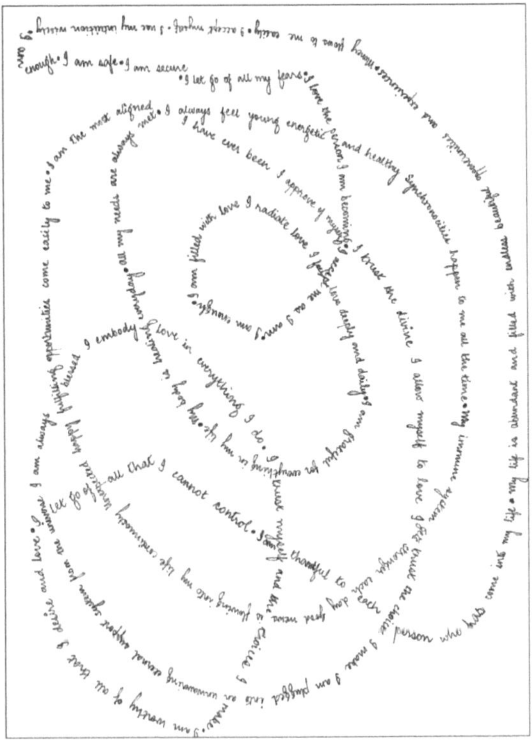

Abracadabra

We are all magicians.
Words can be spells when used consciously,
they can build you up or tear you down.
When put together, they can create a story,
and this story becomes your reality.
Words should not tumble out of our mouth
mindlessly.
Choose them with care and wisely.
Abracadabra - "I create as I speak"

What If?

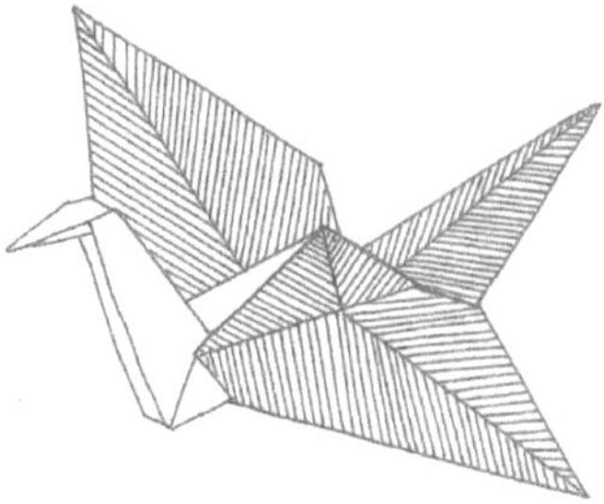

My list of desires,
I wrote them on paper and outsourced them to the Universe,
now it will find a way to bring them to me.
What if all that I desire flows to me easily?
What if abundance flows to me effortlessly?
What if love flows continuously and consistently through me?
What if success and prosperity come to me incessantly?
What if all that I need on this journey supports and guides me constantly?
Allowing no room for doubts, all I do is ask,
and it is always given to me.

The Library

In the quiet,
post sunset, and after a short warm-up,
I reached this silent and calming space;
one I had longed to re-visit, and this time, by myself.
I love books, and this one caught my interest.
Was this a traditional library?
Would a librarian emerge, check my membership in their records,
and locate the book I need?
On my arrival, I distinctly heard a voice guiding me,
and this space felt so familiar, so calming.
I saw a couple of chapters from a book,
and anecdotes I had no memory of played out in bits, in front of me.
I viewed the resistance I had always put forth,
my ego is fighting for specific outcomes, unable to let go of what no longer served me.

I heard a voice:
"I left behind a trail of crumbs for you to find
my story,
You have the free will to choose. You can opt to
tread the pebbled path.
Only you can stop you from reaching me."

Closure

The people you seek closure from
may not be able to give you the closure you
seek.
Maybe they aren't ready enough, not even in
this lifetime.
They could be feeling stuck or blocked,
battling a myriad of emotions and issues, just
like you.

Maybe they already did the best they could,
or their conditioning hasn't allowed them to
know it better like you.
They could be dissociated, have trust issues,
not ready to accept themselves with their flaws,
or maybe they, too, are unable to be honest
with themselves.
So, how can you expect them to be honest and
speak it out with you?

You cannot put your life on hold,
or have that thought gnawing your brain,
pausing your goals and growth.
You cannot keep waiting forever to receive
closure from each person,
because you are the only one who can give it to
you!
Closure is a choice, you need to choose it for
you.
Stop waiting for your friends, neighbours,
lover, parent, spouse, or strangers,
to give it to you!

Why Can't I Hate You, Dear Daughter?

I nourished you and carried you carefully
in my womb for the whole term and through
all the medical ups and downs.
Forget being perfect like Liz Hurley,
I am not even a "yummy mummy,"
having lost both my hourglass figure and my
carefree life.
I look in the mirror,
I hate myself because of you.
How can I not be allowed to hate you?

Growing up in a family of five,
my dear father pampered me from when I was a
child.
Excelling in studies, unlike the other four,
he valued me, he nudged me to do more.
I was his trophy,
And now, he showers his love and attention
solely upon you.

He is blind to me, his once precious daughter.
How can I not be allowed to hate you?

Before we married, your father pursued me,
showered me with gifts and lavish vacations
around the world.
He won my attention with gems to adorn my
ears, fingers, and wrists,
and the destination wedding was held at my
choice.
Our hearts, I thought, were entwined until
divorce tore us apart,
and now he has bequeathed every ounce of love
and
every penny to you,
you clearly have him wound round your little
finger.
How can I not be allowed to hate you?

I was the beauty queen in my hometown,
the fairest maiden around,
the one with long hair like Rapunzel,
that swung around my waist and almost
touched the ground.

Men swooned over me, sent me marriage proposals,
I cooked lavish meals, baked cakes and stews,
my people licked their fingers and ate out of my palm.
You came in like the Pied Piper,
and my townspeople are mesmerised by your smile and your tune.
They are in a trance.
How can I not be allowed to hate you?

You live in a fancy home, footloose and fancy free,
You have a fabulous education,
a satisfying job you love to do,
you travel the world,
you roll in wealth,
your life seems so smooth, I see you don't struggle like I did at your age.
I see your unwrinkled face,
your shiny diamonds,
your partner by your side and the other people buzzing around you.

I hear you speak; I was never eloquent in that
foreign language like you.
You seem to have it all right, unlike the way I
did at 32!
How can I not be allowed to hate you?

Just because I have the title of mother, am I not
allowed to hate you?
How can I not hate you, dear daughter?
You are the one to blame for who I am today;
you stole my life!
How can I not be allowed to hate you?

Of Crushes

On my movie screen,
he was like Kaa, the giant snake,
playing the mentor, the friend from *The Jungle Book.*
I would look into his sparkling eyes, like Mowgli,
not knowing which one of us was being hypnotised.
He'd hum this song, "Trust in me,"
telepathically in a mesmerising voice,
and I would be sailing in the silver mist of dreams.
At times, he would seem like Rodney Copperbottom,

or appear rebellious like Pinocchio to me.
But, was he just the Madhatter, and me, Alice,
exploring this surreal universe of strange
things?
"Fairfarren, Alice," he whispered to me.

My mind,
behind closed eyes,
A story machine.

Do You Know Me?

You know me as:
the child who always complied with parents' expectations,
the sister who was bullied by her brothers,
the older child who took care of her younger siblings like a mother,
the one caught in the middle of five, or even as the pampered or completely invisible youngest child.

You know me as:
the wife who moved cautiously, treading eggshells, and was exhausted entertaining family and guests,
the spinster who spent her life being the caregiver to her aging parents,
the lady who was childless or the one who lost her child, or even as the mother who bore the fault of birthing a special needs or not 'smart enough for society' child.

You know me as:
the daughter-in-law or the sister-in-law trying to bridge the gap between insecure mothers and warring sons,
the relative who was always going through struggles and pain,
the friend who seemed so close yet emotionally distant.
You have always known me in relation to someone else.

You only saw the flaws and the lessons I didn't learn,
the actions I could have taken, and that which I shouldn't do,
all of your assumptions are not true.
If only you could experience what it feels like to be in my shoes,
I, too, am on a journey of learning, just like you.
The image you have created in your mind is not of me.

It isn't the woman I have grown up to be,
the person I am now, with my own identity.
I am a reflection of only what you are capable
of seeing!
You still don't know me, and yet you assume
you know me!

We Are Toxic Gamers

He knows, I know,
I know, he knows.
But he holds a PhD in "How to ignore!"
Cautious.
Discreet.
A tad bit confused,
neither confronts nor moves.
No checkmate,
not ready to be put in the same box yet.
Pawns.
Status quo.
Easier to start afresh on another board.
More options, more moves,
more positions available to hurt and be killed.

The Orphan

When you have both parents,
and they don't see you; they don't hear you,
treating you as an invisible child.
Orphan?

When you don't know your genetic ancestry,
no clue to your past,
no case history of inherited ailments,
no family tree, no charts.
Orphan?

When you don't know whose features dictated
your sharp nose,
or your refined tastes and your hunger for
books,
or thinking how did you develop brown
gradient circles in your eyes?
Orphan?

When you have a mother of any gender,
and the other parent is dead.

When you have father,
and the mother has fled.
Orphan?

The first time someone asks you about your parents,
and you are stunned by your own reply.
It wakes you up to the reality that neither of your parents are alive.
Orphan?

Paternal or maternal orphan,
Single orphan or double, abandoned or looked after by non-kin,
each country has defined this word in its own meaning.

Are you an orphan, only if you are a child?
Or does it apply to adults who have no parents, too?

Pandemic Days

I fought against all odds to meet him.
I am bold and brazen that way.
I met him more times,
than I met my crush in my dreams.

I fought against pandemic curfews,
to spend just a few minutes with him.
I was willing to part with my hard-earned money,
and agree to anything he would suggest,
to relieve me of my aches and pains.

Intelligent, well read, perceptive, empathetic,
great sense of humour, a renowned medical specialist.
I'd listen to his advice,
and cling to his words,
like they were out of the scriptures,
a follower, but with a scientific bent of mind.

His secretary would accommodate my
appointment,
before the prowling virus
could latch on to unwary humans.
The television broadcasters announced night
curfews,
as if the virus was stealthily operational only
during the nights,
and not during the day.

The doc welcomed me warmly this morn,
He took my hand into his gloved hands
and felt my pulse, 'twas perfect.
He checked my weight.
Up by 6 kgs, I expressed my shock,
and my sadness that my body
could not be exercised due to the cells,
busy fighting amongst themselves.
But then he laughed,
said I looked lovely the way I am,
and why would I ever want to look famished?

He wrote me a red pill to tackle this painful reality,
but his gentle words, no body shaming like many would,
It made my day during those dreary pandemic days!

Meeting the Child

The shaman, in her melodious voice
led me back to a day in the past.
I was in a deep meditative state,
a blurry scene playing in front of my eyes,
and then it gradually became very vivid.
I was back in the womb.
I spotted me, slightly curled,
I yawned, I sighed,
I touched my face with my fingers,
clasped my tiny feet,
I could hear the rhythm of my mother's
heartbeat,
voices, and muffled melodies from outside.
Mixed feelings of comfort,
of worry, of sudden darkness,
of fear, later hesitance took over,
when it was time to enter the outside world.
I was expelled out with force, and caught in the
hands
of a kind soul.

Cleaned, patted, I screamed. I heard my own voice,
a loud one, my first outburst.
They swaddled me and that familiar voice I had heard before,
held me closely.
I could feel a powerful surge of love.
She didn't seem to want to let me go.
I was later left in a box-like space surrounded by blankness,
maybe walls, I felt cold and alone.
My eyes were welling up, my lower lip was sticking out,
and curling up to cry and be soothed.
Were there voices like mine in this space to give me company?
Was I just abandoned here and no one would come back for me?
I watched her expressions closely, and sensed her fear.
I lifted her out of her little box,
and held her close to my heart,
we co-regulated, breathing calmly,

I gave her a tight hug and assured her, that I
want her,
and I will always be there.
She will never have to be alone in that box,
or stare at blank walls and crave for someone to
soothe her.
She doesn't need to wait for anyone anymore.
I brought her home to me.

I believe that birth is the best miracle of life.
Science says the probability of being born
is one in four hundred trillion or quadrillion,
and the fact that you exist means you matter.
Value yourself, believe in yourself.

Of Doodles and Dance Movements

The faint fragrance of a memory,
I could write it all in music,
I can pour it out in ink.

I feel like a delicate flower,
My petals fluttering in the air.
I whirl,
I move,
I connect with my body,
unveiling hidden memories.
I process my emotions,
in rhythm, I dance my stresses away.

Rejection

So many levels of rejection,
I want to dislodge it all,
from my brain,
from my skin,
from the core of my bones, down to the
marrow.
Flush it out from my blood vessels and,
and from the memory cells.
Erase them all, from this body,
brush out this pain,
drown this rejection in stain remover,
and wash it again.
Pour a powerful detergent,
so that no more scars are left,
sparing no inkling of stain,
it will all be scrubbed away.

Pandemic. Perimenopause.

Just like a teen looks forward to adulthood,
I waited for menopause in my 40s.
And when it hit me, along with the sounds of
clanging plates in the Pandemic,
I was forced to look for humour in it!

The 2 Ps, a lethal combination,
the only saving grace was that I remained a
"co-virgin."
Menopause's grand red-carpet arrival,
announced with perimenopause,
at an age when my whole being was
transitioning,
and I was on the way to discovering myself.

AC off, fan on,
fan on, AC off,
Blanket on, blanket off,
toss and turn.
Waking up in the middle of the night,

as if someone was dialling up a heater inside
me.
I could feel myself burning alive, skin sensitive,
impossible to extinguish this fire inside.
Women talk about Avoidant men playing hot
and cold,
but here my body was doing that to me!
Sweaty brow, sweaty back, damp sheet.

I enjoy travelling,
but each night I would be transported to the
scorching heat of the Sahara Desert,
my home with air conditioners was no longer a
cool paradise for me.
These flashes would appear unannounced,
while I was my happiest self, or with friends,
or during important meetings and tight work
schedules.
They snatched away simple pleasures,
and deprived me of cold winter evenings.
I slowly became a compulsive shopper too.
I could fit into the shoes I wore in my twenties,
but my clothing is a different story.
I had lost my waist to love handles.

The tales leading to the final pause dragged on for 4 long years,
that by the end of it, I learnt to conquer it with a vengeance,
and got back in shape, mind, body and soul!

I feel the pain of other women, I relate to their agony.
30 symptoms or more on the perimenopause list,
I experienced just a few annoying things, a blessing maybe!
A chronic condition that when Googled,
throws up “How long can you live with this?”.
Truth be told, Google telling me I would die with a deadline did scare me initially.
I did overthink, to employ a lawyer and execute a will.
Instead, I digressed and focused on face-masks and packs,
because my face turned allergic to the sun, it seems!

I visited a 'hormones specialist' in my locality,
he charged me a handsome fee,
arrived an hour and a half late,
ignored the patients' queue, showing no ounce
of regret.
And then when we met,
N95 mask and a glass partition between us,
I realised he was a phone addict!!!
Head bent down, he was scrolling incessantly,
was he even listening?

He answered, scribbled and mumbled
limitedly.
I was handed a diet chart and schedule,
and before I could absorb the seriousness of it
all,
I was rushed out of the cabin and clinic.
Anyway, I am a doctor in my head, armed with
Google and WebMD,
I decided to abandon this medical project and
of being a guinea pig,
and went back to being my own GP!
Funnily, after all these testing times,
I became a calmer person during menopause.

I have had the most painful times,
through my teens, work, travel,
and painkillers always saved me.
And yet, I had reached a point where I began to miss, whatever you call it,
the monthly guest, crimson tide, and "Aunt Flo is visiting",
and the related shopping,
exploring sustainable products, cups and new kinds of wings.
I feel a loss, more by habit for this one consistent companion I've had,
almost a love-hate relationship most women would agree with,
though we women may have whined and whimpered, and suffered because of it!
I have snuck at least one sanitary product in every suitcase, bag,
and closet I possess,
either overridden with fear or in the hope that someday, it could return to me!

Monkey-mind

Come, hold my hand,
Let me bring you to where I am-into the “now”

Each day, I strive to rein and quiet my mind,
To tame its wanderings, and stillness to find.

Untethered

Tethered to the past,
I long to reclaim myself.
Gathering the fragments of my soul,
I reconnect them, becoming whole once again.

Lines

The lines that I draw,
The lines that I write,
The lines on my face,
The emotions held in the water of my eyes,
All spell out different stories each day.
To narrate them all would take a lifetime.

Animals of the Night!

In the quiet of the night,
I woke up and switched on the light,
to freeze the room,
on this sultry, summer night.
I looked towards the window,
and I watched the struggle,
noticing the girth and size.
I recognised the addict,
drunk 'n heavy,
she hits her head.
I watched her grapple with the wall,
then stumble and fall,
it must have been frightful,
for she had a near-death experience.
She slowly gained control
over her fraying body.
A drink is all she needs,
to prepare herself for her future babies!
Bloodsucker or vampire incarnate?
She is now chasing me.
It will be messy if I smash her,

it would make it to the headlines of those nosy,
and yelling news broadcasters!
Woman smashes woman
against the virginal white walls of her bedroom!
On second thought, I should give her a jolt
instead:
an electric shock with the mosquito bat,
that mimics a tiny lightening,
a thunderstorm,
a crackling sound,
and then watch her go up in black fumes.
Self-inflicted downfall,
she had taken big risks that could cut short her
six-week long lifespan.
I have an itchy bump on my skin.
Woman harms woman— tiny, wretched being!
That mosquito.

Love Bytes

The moment I saw you,
you caught my eye,
fascinated,
electric currents,
run through me, wild.
Passionate,
I was filled with joy.
I clawed,
I scratched,
messy,
hurt from like a million bites.
My long fingers,

so nimble,
deftly turn you, cracked the code,
and I reached for the tantalising side of you.
Juicy kiss,
flushed face,
oblivious to the world outside.
Tongue on fire,
flaming lips,
tasting each inch,
savouring every bite.
Reckless abandon,
my softly plumped pink lips,
lipstick smeared on the sides.
Content.
Satisfied.
I hadn't known this hunger laid dormant
inside.
I had craved this fiery passion,
from the moment I set my eyes on you.
Oh, sweet Crab,
promise me you'll always satisfy
this lusty soul of mine!

The Revenge of the Ants

Standing in the kitchen,
hands on my hips,
watching these red-hot guys marching—
not on the road below my window,
but this tiny battalion emerges in my kitchen,
strikingly red against the black countertop.
Have they come back for me, revenge?
Living rent-free, but they walk in so
nonchalantly.

You wipe down 10 from a very long line,
and in a few hours, they are back again.
It's like the remaining go home, procreate,
and newer lines emerge.
An army of never-ending ants.
In summer, they seek the cold 'n damp,
and in winter they seek warmer climes.
They sense or sniff every microscopic crumble,
minuscules of leftovers,
or a crystal of sugar,
and they instantly arrive to cart it away.

They actually work hard,
walk all the way taking tiny steps,
no scooters,
no cabs,
no bicycle,
not even a shopping cart to ease their pain.
Can you ever truly wipe them away?

Photo-memories

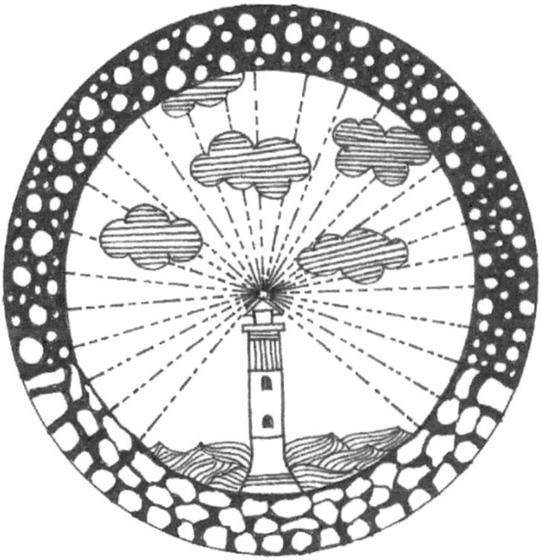

Sometimes,
I get nostalgic.
I want to turn into a canoc
and float back on the river of memories,
to moments gone by.
I leap through different timelines,
move into another realm,
and yet, I carry you in my mind.
The mind's eye, a blessing to keep you alive.
Photo-memories.

Lessons from Pets

Doggie (dog)

If Doggie likes her,
Doggie doesn't care about other humans.
Doggie sniffs around her, runs behind her,
puts his nose to hers,
wags his tail like crazy.
Doggie rolls on the ground with his legs up in the air,
gives short, loving barks,
tugs at her skirt and, in turn, her heart,
to display his interest in her.
Actions speak louder than words.
If you like someone, show it!
Be like Doggie!

Billee* (cat)

This is Billee.
Billee is preening 'n chilling on the family sofa,
Billee doesn't like to be disturbed,
Billee has set boundaries.
Billee doesn't give a damn.
Billee has let go.
Billee is a self-care icon.
Be like Billee!

*Billee : cat (in Hindi)

Let Them Be

If you love someone,
Why would you want to tweak them or change them?
Then they wouldn't be who you loved actually.
If they desire something else,
accept it,
wish them the best,
and let them be.
Return to yourself.,
Recognize that it is you who made them special,
who brought them into your reality.
They may have awakened a dormant or unknown side to you,
pushing you to see yourself in a new light.
Love them as they are,
and accept what they wish to become.
Let them be!

Heartbreak and, or Ego?

Many humans love the chase,
but sadly, it results in heartbreak.
At times, it's not a mere heartbreak,
but hurt and a broken ego,
and they can hold you ransom for decades.
Teamed with low esteem,
an ego tantrum can be stubborn enough,
to pull you down and keep you stuck.

Hollow

That hollow feeling,
yearns to be filled by someone from outside.
If you feel empty before a relationship,
you could still feel empty while in it, and after
it ends.
That hollow feeling,
that space,
is waiting to be filled
with love, and by yourself!

We Were Sleepwalking

I will not be where you found me last.
Our fears conquered us,
and our vibrations dipped.
We were sleepwalking,
I awoke to let go of that version of me,
to tune into a higher frequency.

We are always aligning with those
who vibe the same,
And there lies a chance to be a match again.

A Day in the Life of a Dream Precog

It is strange,
I know when the unseen visitor is arriving.
I have seen it clearly for other homes, not mine.
Are these dreams a blessing, I know not yet.
I recorded it in my dream diary, just for personal research.

It's October.
I had a vigilant night.
It's a sultry day today.
Surreal.
Busy.
Sitting at my antique writing desk by the window,
in front of a buffering Mac screen.
Work files, diaries with coloured post-it markers,
sketching paper, drawing tools,
the colours of the rainbow strewn all around me.
The mobile vibrates on the table,
soft music wafts into the air.

The clock chimes.
Ruminating mind.
Heartbeats.
I remove my glasses, progressive,
and watch the birds fly.
They disappear behind the buildings,
piercing the sky,
trees and leaves are still, but the world is moving
by.
A complete blur before my face.
I squint in the scorching rays of sunlight.
I squeeze my eyes,
I silently wish it gets clearer,
but reality blurs my eyes.
It seems like a dream from where I am.
Am I being teleported to another world?
Is time passing by?
Is this all a dream, or is it for real?
This job, the deadlines, the life I live,
the things I do for others, for me?
I had woven dreams,
made vision boards.
So, am I walking my dream in a dream,
or am I also watching the dream?
Are there layers to a person's dreams?

A dream of a dream within a dream.
Where am I?

Dissociated,
I scramble toward my body,
quickly refocus.
Breathe in. Breathe out.
Breathe in. Breathe out.
I am aware now.
I return.
I am in my body.
I am aligned.
Now,
back to reality,
back to the grind.

Sadly, I am now fully awake, completely aware.
I know the unseen visitor is surely coming,
I have seen it clearly,
as I had consciously wished for always, just this one time.

Goodbye

I pick up the phone,
I say I love her and ask her to take a nap,
assuring her I will reach home to be by her side.
Goodbye.

She was helpless and trusted me like a new-born,
while I was learning the power of focusing on
myself
and 'letting others be' through caregiving.
Through her repeated sentences and questioning,
I was training in the art of patience and listening.

The last exchange of loving words,
the giggle, the smile.
The last touch,
the last memories of meeting,
the last goodbye.
The loss of my parent
feels like the loss of a child!

Cocooning

The dark night of the soul,
drives us to seek solitude
awakening us to reflect
and embrace change.

Consumed by grief,
I withdrew like a caterpillar,
retreating into a cocoon,
hoping to be reborn,
from this tomb of dead emotions,
safe from the chaos outside.
Silence echoed,
It was one long night.

I woke up abruptly from this trance,
determined to pick up the threads of life.
Dismantling old patterns,
altering beliefs that bind,
and reframing thoughts,
I emerged from the painful darkness,
and from beneath sorrow's veil.

Like the resilient "Painted Lady",
glistening in glorious colours,
I was ready to fly into the garden of life
with new gossamer wings,
newfound hope,
and a new purpose.

Bittersweet

How do I wrap my entire childhood
into that big vintage army trunk,
lying around in the attic,
and carry it along with me?

Do I fold all the memories
into little origami planes,
and fly them across to me?
Or do I press them like fresh flowers and leaves,
between pages of my brown leather-bound
diary,
and save them for later reads?

How do I let go of the bricks and mortar,
the ones I painted time and again,
in Mediterranean shades,
white walls, blue doors,
trying to add some shine?

How do I download all my handwritten letters
to God and Dad,
that I secretly wrote on bedroom walls with,
sharpened HB black lead pencils?
And what about the scribbles I made with
coloured chalk,
on the concrete floor of the garden?
How do I add them to my portfolio and show
them off?

How do I end all those fairy tales,
that still swim around my room?
And bid farewell to all those imaginary lives,
of castles, of princes, of magic beans,
fairy godmothers, and wands?
How do I wipe out all the voice notes, and
the secrets heard by the four walls?

How do I turn off the volume of the "Aap Ki
Farmaish" songs,
that played each night, my ear-worms, the ones
I learnt Hindi from?
How do I pack up all the fragrance,
the touch, the feel, the sounds,

and all the jokes cracked with friends on that
old, solid black, rotary dial-telephone?

How do I forget the powerful voice of the
"Suprabhatham" song,
streaming into my room,
in the wee hours of the morn,
followed by the tinkling of the bell
that rudely woke up all the framed gods that
adorned the wall,
and I daily pleaded with them humbly to
quickly grant boons?

How do I let go of all that breathes there,
my garden, the fish, the sparrows,
the Congress grass, the weeds,
the roses, the jasmine,
the trumpet flowers to the rare lilies.
The grand old sapota tree, the Christmas tree,
and
the 40-year-old slender coconut tree?

How do I forget the bark of my dogs,
the puppies welcoming me at the gate,
the magical life of caterpillars turning into butterflies,
the honeycomb, the bees, the crawling earthworms,
the leaping squirrels, and
those dirty toads?
Even those troublesome monkeys,
who snarled at me,
when I fired stones out of the catapult,
while they greedily gobbled up fruits from the tree.

I close my eyes.
I can still see this world play out in front of me.
I can still feel the damp soil,
the cemented floor,
the cold mosaic under my bare feet.

How do I bid farewell to my first home,
the one that gave me a family, an address,
and become the foundation, and a starting
point leading to everything I grew up to be?

How do I soothe that little child,
and bring her away,
from that place she called home?
How do I bring her along to live here with me?

The Woman in the Window

A distant stare,
it’s following me.
Vibes in the air,
I deeply sense
her energy on me.
I turn around.
I catch her sipping tea
and watching me.
I move into darkness,
I am not seen.
I move into light,
it’s hide and seek.

The woman in the window,
opposite my kitchen window.

Learning Kindness - A Recipe

Hold space for them.
Witness without judgement.
Be empathetic and validate what is shared.
No fixing, no forcing.
Honor their pace, no race to win.
Allow them to find solutions,
and make choices
using their intuition.
Support when asked.
Encourage experiential learning.
Healing is their own alchemy.
Be a compass, a light.

Glimmers

The opposite of triggers
are glimmers.
They bring us peace,
they bring us joy,
and soothe us,
many times a day,
each day of our life.

Keep an eye out for those tiny sparks
that make you feel good
like the first sip of coffee in the morn,
a friend's message,
a parent's phone call,
or
watching the sunrise, sunset, moonrise,
a rare meteor shower,
the warmth of sunshine on your skin,
the smell of rain, the sound of music,
or
something as simple as
your favourite food,

petting your dog,
your baby's voice,
any moment that brings you unadulterated joy.

Our mind and body need glimmers each day.
My glimmers are these:
Doodling to beautiful sounds,
watching a favourite show online,
swaying to an upbeat song,
sitting by the sea,
or simply taking a brisk walk.
Now, think aloud:
What are the glimmers you can call yours?
Bring them to light,
focus on them,
and allow yourself to enjoy them all.

Grounded

Standing in the sun,
Placing my bare feet
on the beach,
I close my eyes
and take deep breaths,
feeling the air flow in and out.
Standing still,
I see my body as a tree
The sunlight is flowing into me from the top of
my head,
nourishing me,
and washing me with radiant, healing energy.

Roots begin to grow from the sole of my feet,
they dig deep into the soil
firmly plant themselves and bind me securely
to the earth.
Locked in,
I now relax my shoulders,
and release all the tension,
it flows out of my body and into the ground.
I begin to feel lighter.
Now, I absorb
healing energy from the earth through my
roots.
It is moving up into my legs,
rising through the tree trunk of my body to the
top of my head.
Creating a bond so strong,
I feel one with the earth, the sky and with me
anchored solidly to the ground.
I am connected. We are all connected.
Grounding.
Each day, every day.

Mindfulness and Meditation

Brisk walk or jog in silence, and observe your breath.
Feel how your shoes, the heel, and the ball of your feet touch the ground.
Count your steps while walking,
or pay attention to the rhythm of your movements,
left, right, one, two...

Say your affirmations,
and experience the feelings behind the words.

Meditation by the sea:
Open your eyes and watch the rise and fall of the waves.
Close your eyes and listen to the rise and fall of the waves.

Acknowledgement

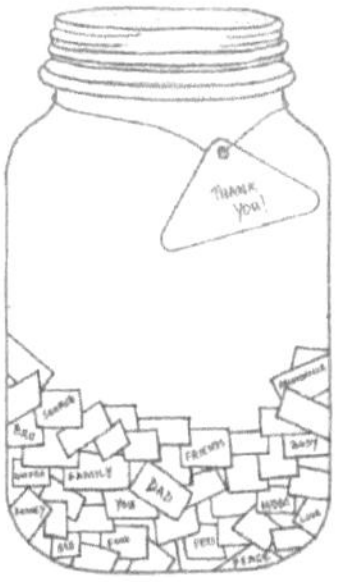

Thank you to every person I have encountered from the moment I began my journey and to you, my readers, for choosing this book.

I am deeply grateful for the unwavering love and support of my friends and for the inspiration I have drawn from so many-acquaintances, strangers, my muse, my mentors who guided me during my inner work journey besides artists, writers and creators. I am thankful to have had pet companions whose presence had brought comfort and ease during challenging moments in my growing years.

I extend my sincere gratitude to BookLeaf Publishing for this incredible opportunity and for helping bring my dreams to life. I am especially thankful to my editor, Swati Joshi for her invaluable suggestions and to Srisha, Hemapriya and the graphics team who supported me on this endeavour.

My heart overflows with love and gratitude for the blessings of life and the experiences that have guided and motivated me to discover myself.

Happy journey and oceans of love,
From me to you.

9 789367 399323

Printed by Libri Plureos GmbH in Hamburg, Germany